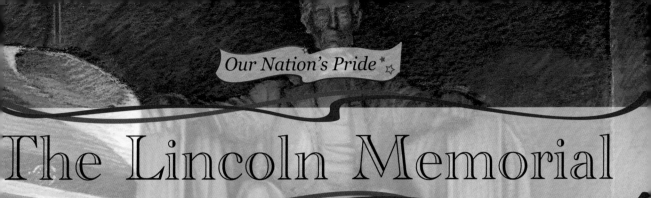

Our Nation's Pride

The Lincoln Memorial

By Karen Latchana Kenney
Illustrated by Judith A. Hunt

Content Consultant:
Richard Jensen, PhD
Author, Scholar, and Historian

magic
Wagon

visit us at www.abdopublishing.com

Published by Magic Wagon, a division of the ABDO Group, 8000 West 78th Street, Edina, Minnesota, 55439. Copyright © 2011 by Abdo Consulting Group, Inc. International copyrights reserved in all countries. All rights reserved. No part of this book may be reproduced in any form without written permission from the publisher.

Looking Glass Library™ is a trademark and logo of Magic Wagon.

Printed in the United States of America, North Mankato, Minnesota.
092010
012011

 THIS BOOK CONTAINS AT LEAST 10% RECYCLED MATERIALS.

Text by Karen Latchana Kenney
Illustrations by Judith A. Hunt
Edited by Melissa Johnson
Interior layout and design by Becky Daum
Cover design by Becky Daum

Library of Congress Cataloging-in-Publication Data
Kenney, Karen Latchana.
  The Lincoln Memorial / by Karen Latchana Kenney ; illustrated by Judith A. Hunt.
     p. cm. — (Our nation's pride)
  Includes index.
  ISBN 978-1-61641-151-0
  1. Lincoln Memorial (Washington, D.C.)—Juvenile literature. 2. Lincoln, Abraham, 1809-1865—Monuments—Washington (D.C.)—Juvenile literature. 3. Washington (D.C.)—Buildings, structures, etc.—Juvenile literature. I. Hunt, Judith A., 1955- ill. II. Title.
  F203.4.L73K45 2011
  975.3--dc22
                        2010013996

Table of Contents

A Man in Thought

At the edge of a reflecting pool stands a shining white building. People walk up its long stairs. They go past its tall columns. Inside, they find a huge statue of a man sitting in a chair. He looks like he is thinking about something important.

This man is President Abraham Lincoln. The building is the Lincoln Memorial in Washington DC. People come to this special place to remember this great president.

The Sixteenth President

Abraham Lincoln became president during a difficult time in U.S. history. In 1861, many people in southern states owned slaves. People in the northern states thought all people should be free.

Lincoln was from the North. Some people in the southern states feared that he would end slavery. They decided to become a separate country. Lincoln wanted the United States to stay as one. This started the American Civil War.

A President Dies

After many battles, the North won the American Civil War. President Lincoln kept the United States together. He made the end of slavery possible.

On April 14, 1865, President Lincoln went to see a play. At the theater, the president was shot. John Wilkes Booth was angry the North had won the war. So, he killed the president. People across the country mourned the death of their leader.

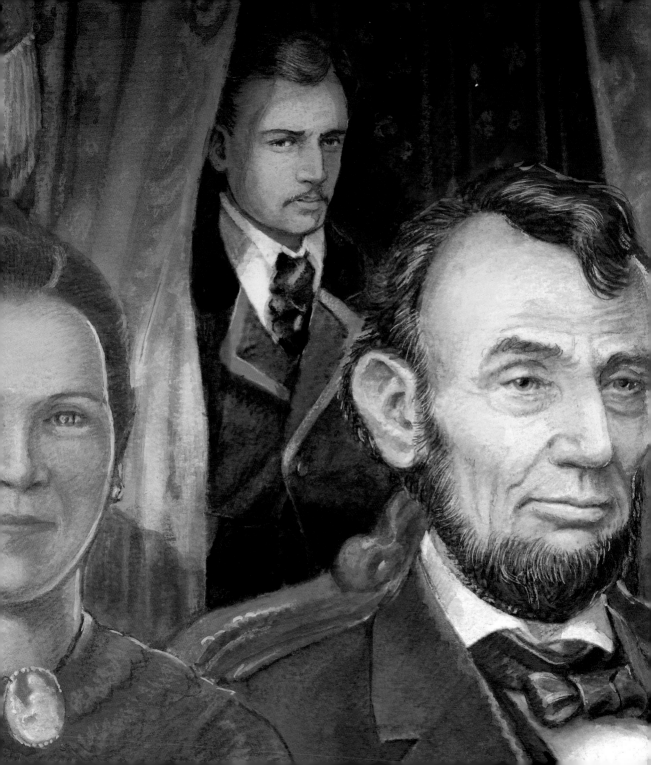

A Plan for a Memorial

Americans wanted to honor the president.

The government decided to make a memorial

to remember Lincoln. In 1911, the plan for the

memorial was chosen. It was based on a famous

temple in Greece.

The Statue

The memorial needed a statue of the president.

Daniel Chester French was hired to create it. French

studied photographs and drawings of Lincoln.

He practiced by making a model of the statue.

Lincoln would look strong, wise, and kind.

Then, the model had to be made into a giant

statue. Carvers cut 28 blocks of white marble. Next,

workers put the blocks together. The statue looked

like one smooth piece of marble.

Building the Memorial

In 1914, work started on the base of the memorial. Workers dug holes in the soft land. They filled the holes with steel and concrete. This made the building strong.

The walls and columns were made of different types of stone. Outside the memorial, workers built a long pool. The pool would reflect the beautiful white building. After years of hard work, the memorial was completed in 1922.

Lincoln's First Speech

Important words are carved in the memorial's walls. They are two speeches made by President Lincoln. The first is the Gettysburg Address. In this speech, Lincoln spoke about freedom and keeping the country together.

Above this speech is a painting. It shows an angel with slaves in chains. The angel is taking off their chains. The painting means freedom and liberty, just like the Gettysburg Address.

...ACE FOR THOSE WHO HERE GAVE
THEIR LIVES THAT THAT NATION
MIGHT LIVE . IT IS ALTOGETHER FIT-
TING AND PROPER THAT WE SHOULD
DO THIS . BUT IN A LARGER SENSE
WE CAN NOT DEDICATE- WE CAN NOT
CONSECRATE- WE CAN NOT HALLOW-
THIS GROUND . THE BRAVE MEN LIV-
ING AND DEAD WHO STRUGGLED HERE
HAVE CONSECRATED IT FAR ABOVE
OUR POOR POWER TO ADD OR DETRACT
THE WORLD WILL LITTLE NOTE NOR
LONG REMEMBER WHAT WE SAY HERE
BUT IT CAN NEVER FORGET WHAT THEY
DID HERE . IT IS FOR US THE LIVING
RATHER TO BE DEDICATED HERE TO
THE UNFINISHED WORK WHICH THEY
WHO FOUGHT HERE HAVE THUS FAR
SO NOBLY ADVANCED . IT IS RATHER FOR
US TO BE HERE DEDICATED TO THE
GREAT TASK REMAINING BEFORE US-
THAT FROM THESE HONORED DEAD
WE TAKE INCREASED DEVOTION TO
THAT CAUSE FOR WHICH THEY GAVE THE
LAST FULL MEASURE OF DEVOTION-
THAT WE HERE HIGHLY RESOLVE THAT
THESE DEAD SHALL NOT HAVE DIED IN
VAIN- THAT THIS NATION UNDER GOD
SHALL HAVE A NEW BIRTH OF FREEDOM-
AND THAT GOVERNMENT OF THE PEOPLE
BY THE PEOPLE FOR THE PEOPLE SHALL
NOT PERISH FROM THE EARTH

Lincoln's Second Speech

The second speech is carved on the other side of the statue. Lincoln gave this speech after he became president for the second time. He spoke about people who died in the war. He spoke about fighting until slavery was gone.

Above the speech is a painting. It shows an angel and two people. One person is from the North. The other is from the South. The angel holds their hands together. This painting means unity.

The Memorial's Symbols

Different parts of the Lincoln Memorial are symbols. Around the building are 36 columns. When Lincoln was president, there were 36 states. Each column stands for a state. Written above each column is a state's name. All 36 columns stand together as a symbol of unity.

Many kinds of stone make up the Lincoln

Memorial. Each kind was taken from different

states. There is granite from Massachusetts. Marble

came from Alabama, Georgia, Colorado, and

Tennessee. Limestone was brought from Indiana.

These stones came from the North and the South.

They are another symbol of unity.

Lincoln's hands on the statue are symbols, too.

One hand is open. The other is a fist. The open

hand shows the kindness and fairness of the

president. Lincoln's fist shows how strong he was

during the American Civil War.

"I Have a Dream"

On August 28, 1963, thousands of people marched to the Lincoln Memorial. The American Civil War had been over for almost 100 years. But African Americans were still not treated equally.

Martin Luther King Jr. stood on the steps of the Lincoln Memorial that day. He gave a speech that everyone would remember. It was his "I Have a Dream" speech. The crowd hoped for a time when every American would be treated fairly.

Visiting the
Lincoln Memorial

The Lincoln Memorial is always open, even at night. You can walk through and look at the paintings. Stare up at the statue of President Lincoln. Read his speeches.

During the day, rangers work at the memorial. Ask them questions. Learn about this great president. Think about the important things he did for the United States.

28

Fun Facts

- On May 30, 1922, the Lincoln Memorial was finished. People celebrated at the memorial. Robert Lincoln, President Lincoln's only living son, was there.

- It cost $2,957,000 to build the Lincoln Memorial.

- The statue of Lincoln is very big! Its head alone is taller than the kids who look up at it.

- Look at a U.S. $5 bill and a penny. On one side is a picture of Abraham Lincoln. On the other side is a picture of the Lincoln Memorial. In 2009, a new penny design came out. Instead of the Lincoln Memorial, the new pennies have scenes from Lincoln's life.

Glossary

column—a tall pillar that supports a building.

marble—a hard stone used to make buildings and statues.

memorial—something that is made to remember a person or an event.

mourn—to be sad when a person dies.

reflect—to show an image on a shiny surface.

statue—three-dimensional artwork made of wood, clay, metal, or other hard material.

symbol—something that stands for something else.

unity—the act of joining together to make one group, as in the different states that make the United States.

On the Web

To learn more about the Lincoln Memorial, visit ABDO Group online at **www.abdopublishing.com**. Web sites about the Lincoln Memorial are featured on our Book Links page. These links are routinely monitored and updated to provide the most current information available.

Index